The Mindful Bride

The Calm Way to Your Wedding Day

JOANNE JAMIS CAIN

KDEPittsburgh Publishing

Pittsburgh, PA

THE MINDFUL BRIDE

Paperback ISBN : 979-8-218-59100-7

Cover Photo of Nina by Kelly Nardone Photography
Cover design and formatting:
Karen Captline - betterbecreative.com

Editor: Cally Jamis Vennare - cjvcommunications.com

Website: Mary Jamis

TheMindfulBride.com

Dedicated to

The Brides of
Katherine's Daughter Events
Thank you!

In Memory of

Katherine Jamis,
The Queen of Hospitality
&
Daleen Wilson,
My Biggest Cheerleader

Gratitude to

My Cain Family

Danielle Cunic

Sara Bagiatis

Leah Marino Poplowski

Maria Simbra

The Women of Ironed Words Writing Circle

Rita Rizos Pappas

WHAT IS A "MINDFUL BRIDE?"

*How to maintain a sense of
inner calmness and compassion for all
as you plan your wedding.*

I crafted this little book for the bride who would like to plan a wedding day in a calm and purposeful way. There are certain characteristics of mindfulness that can apply while planning a wedding and these will be shared throughout the book.

No bride should feel that everything about their wedding day must be perfect. The Mindful Bride embodies a sense of presence, calmness, and awareness as best they can throughout the entire wedding process. It's about being attuned to emotions and the experience, savoring each moment rather than being consumed by stress or external expectations.

HERE ARE SOME GUIDELINES AS YOU JOURNEY THROUGH THE BOOK.

Stay calm and live in the moment
Do your best to radiate inner peace, stay grounded, and focus on the present.

Endeavor to be emotionally connected
Embrace your feelings, whether it be excitement, joy, or nervousness.

Practice balance and being present
Focus on the big picture and the purpose of the day. Remain centered on your partner, loved ones, and the significance of the celebration, rather than obsessing over perfection.

Make decisions with a consciousness
From choosing your wedding dress to selecting the venue or décor, do so with thoughtfulness. You might opt for choices that are meaningful, sustainable, or connected to your values.

Show compassion
Mindfulness fosters a deep sense of compassion. Be aware of your own feelings and practice kindness to your family, friends, and anyone involved in the wedding planning process.

Ultimately, The Mindful Bride is focused on the love they share with their partner.

The wedding day is less about the details and more about the connection. Take time to cherish the relationship that led to this moment.

INSIDE THE
MINDFUL BRIDE

There is a whirlwind of emotions and excitement
that comes with saying "yes!" Hear the benefits of good
planning, and learn the difference between a wedding
planner and a day-of coordinator. A detailed master
checklist guides you through every step of the
wedding journey, ensuring you stay organized and
on track from the very beginning.

Let's talk about budgets! Weddings can be expensive,
but you can make financial decisions that reflect your
priorities without breaking the bank. Learn how to
create a realistic budget, allocate funds effectively,
and stick to your plan.

Your special day relies on a team of experts — here's your
ultimate guide to choosing and managing wedding vendors.
From finding the perfect florist and photographer to navigating
contracts, deposits, and timelines, you'll discover how to create
a dream team that aligns with your style and budget.

Learn everything you need to know about selecting
and managing your bridal party. Understand how to
choose the right people and define their roles. Tips
for fostering positive relationships, handling financial
challenges, and balancing personalities help ensure
a supportive and cohesive wedding crew.

Planning a wedding often involves blending dreams,
traditions, and family expectations. Explore how to
navigate the delicate balance between celebrating
your unique love story and honoring the needs of others.
Discover strategies for constructive communication,
making compromises, and setting boundaries to
create a harmonious planning process.

Find the inspiration and tools to design a wedding
that reflects your vision, personality, and love story.
From church or venue ceremonies to reception rooms,
checklists are included that will assist you in planning
each segment of your wedding day.

As you countdown to your wedding day, review
everything from the final walk-through and rehearsal
to creating your timeline. Also included are checklists
for the month leading up to your wedding, and your
"day-of kit" to keep you stress-free.

Delve deeper into your emotional landscape on the
wedding day — a day brimming with excitement, love,
and reflection. From the quiet moments to the
heartwarming joy of marrying your partner, be
reminded of what's most important.

The wedding may be over, but your journey isn't!
Review current post-wedding etiquette, including
thank-you notes. Other newlywed ideas such as
preserving your dress or donating it, and what to do
with leftover décor, are presented.

A beloved wedding tradition for many, cookie tables
are more than just dessert — they're a celebration of
community and heritage. Tips on assembling a
spectacular spread, how many cookies to bake, how
to ensure cookies for everyone, and personalizing your
table are included!

YOU'RE ENGAGED!

The foundation of a calm wedding day is good planning.

*The more decisions you can make early on,
the easier things will be later. Trust me!*

Ah, what a wonderful event has happened in your life — your engagement! You are probably experiencing a range of emotions, am I right? Most new brides tell me they are excited, thrilled, without words, and maybe a bit overwhelmed. May I offer my congratulations on this major event ... and some words of wisdom!

Once the reality of what has happened settles in, many of my brides get super excited about planning their big day. Some already have Pinterest boards created, posts and videos reserved, photos gathered, and vendor referrals saved. Sometimes a proposal is a complete surprise, other times it comes after much discussion and ring selection. Many brides have already thought in advance about their wedding and what the vision of that special day might look like.

How are you feeling about planning your big day? Brides who opt to pay for a planner to design and do *everything* (well, maybe they do pick out their own dress!) are in the minority. More frequently, brides plan their own weddings and opt for the security of a day-of coordinator. The day-of coordinator enters the month or two before the wedding, manages the vendors, and oversees the unfolding of the wedding day – the day that you have carefully planned.

Regardless of whether you hire planning help or not, this little book is for the bride *who wants to be in on her wedding from the word "go."* If you are excited about planning, designing, creating, and putting your stamp on your big day, my hand is in yours. Or, if you are less than excited, not organized, scared a little (or a lot), I'm hugging you and saying it will be alright.

As we go through the chapters together, keep in mind that you are building the foundation of your big day. The more planning you do and the more decisions you make ahead of time, the calmer your day will be.

Everyone is different. What may overwhelm one bride may be a *cake walk* (a bridal metaphor!) for another, and vice versa. A bride once told me that just the thought of everyone's eyes upon her as she walked down the aisle made her very nervous. I could see that even talking about it caused an emotional reaction.

I suggested that when the big moment came, her gaze should only be at her beloved. "You are walking towards the one you love," I reminded her. "That is all that matters at that moment."

"Wow," she said, "You are right!"

So, if any part of this makes you scared, nervous, or upset even thinking about it, we will explore it. Together. This is why I made this little helper of a book — to assist you from the moment that you are engaged, all the way to your wedding day.

A wedding day can be a huge, choreographed event. But

remember this: at its core is the union of two special people, coming together to pledge their love to one another and creating a lifelong memory for years to come.

As founder of Katherine's Daughter Events (KDE) for over a decade, I have been honored to help countless brides with their special day. Oftentimes I work as a cross between a planner and day-of coordinator by providing insight into a wedding's design, logistics, vendor selection, and day-of wedding execution. This book allows me to share my experiences, wisdom, and knowledge with you in what I hope is your personal quest to be The Mindful Bride.

ProTip: *To clarify, a wedding planner is involved in all phases of planning your wedding from vendor selections, site visits, design decisions, and day-of execution. A day-of coordinator usually comes on board a month or two before your wedding date to review contracts, oversee logistics, do a final walkthrough, and attend rehearsal. They are also there on the day of the wedding to make sure things unfold the way they're supposed to, and to be a point of contact for the family, guests, and vendors.*

Your wedding should be the ultimate experience for you and your guests. Do I think you should budget for a wedding planner or day-of coordinator like KDE; yes, I do! Here's why:

The desire for guests to enjoy themselves is a key reason that brides seek my help; most couples, understandably, just want their guests to have a good time. *Managing the extensive amount of detail (and expense!) associated with a wedding* is another top motivator for hiring a wedding planner. *An assurance that the family and bridal party can relax and enjoy the day of the wedding* — instead of decorating tables, fine tuning the décor, and stressing that all is in place at the venue — is also a frequent request from my brides.

Good planning is the foundation of a calm wedding day for The Mindful Bride. Making important decisions early on ensures a memorable and beautiful wedding day for you. Guidance can come from many sources – online resources, a professional wedding planner or a day-of coordinator, and this little book!

Years ago, my mother planned my wedding. I picked out my dress, by myself, because mom was working, and my sisters were away at college. Maybe I didn't expect to buy a dress that day, but I had a bridal magazine. I pointed to a picture, and I think my gown was the second one I tried on.

After that, I remember making white Jordan almond favors tied with a bow with my two sisters. I picked out dresses and baskets of silk flowers for my bridesmaids. Other than that, I don't remember much else. My mother must have planned the invitations, catering, table set ups, and the band. I had a big Greek wedding with live music, and it was a blast.

These days, not many mothers plan weddings; couples are the ones who do most of the planning. Mothers often get relegated to a singular duty, such as coordinating a cookie table (see my bonus section!) or helping with the design or wedding theme.

But mothers DO influence what goes on at the wedding, especially with younger couples who may also need parental support (emotional and/or financial) for decisions about venue, photographer, music, flowers, catering, etc.

Older couples tend to be more established and financially in a position to pay, so they like to make many of their own decisions without (or despite) family suggestions. These are not hard and fast rules. But there can be some tricky monetary things that go on when couples accept help from families. I will discuss this area in more detail in the *Celebration and Compromise* section.

I will do my best to address as many challenges, options, and parts of a wedding day that I can in this book. Feel free to read any part of it at any time, depending on what stage of the process you may be experiencing now. Remember that advance planning and decisions will make your life much easier. Also remember to seek out extra advice when you feel that you need more information. There's lots of research on the internet that can be had with just a little bit of time and effort.

Ready to get started?

Here we go!

Master Timeline for The Mindful Bride
Use whatever applies to you. Check off the blocks as you go!

8-12 months (or whenever you get started!)

- ❒ Announce your engagement.
- ❒ Set a wedding date.
- ❒ Decide on an overall budget.
- ❒ Book your venue.
- ❒ Book your church or officiant.
- ❒ Book your photographer, videographer, DJ, and caterer.
- ❒ Decide if you'll have a wedding planner or a day-of coordinator.
- ❒ Book any extra vendors such as transportation, bakery, photo booth, florist, child and pet care, hair and makeup.
- ❒ Research hotel room blocks.
- ❒ Take engagement photos.
- ❒ Order "Save the Date" invitations.
- ❒ Buy your dress.
- ❒ Choose your bridal party.
- ❒ Assist bridesmaids with color choice and style of their attire.
- ❒ Remind groomsmen to reserve a suit or tux.
- ❒ Make honeymoon plans.
- ❒ Create a Pinterest board with your style ideas.
- ❒ Start your guest list.
- ❒ Plan your bridal shower.
- ❒ Look at invitations and narrow down choices.
- ❒ Take a weekend away with girlfriends or your fiance, just to rest.

6-8 months

- ❏ Send "Save the Dates."
- ❏ Shop for wedding bands.
- ❏ Investigate wedding license requirements for your area.
- ❏ Apply for or renew your passports.
- ❏ Decide on your wedding decor (signage, favors, memorial table) and begin ordering props.
- ❏ Develop a transportation plan for guests to/from hotel and book shuttle or bus if necessary.
- ❏ Finalize guest list.
- ❏ Book rehearsal dinner location.
- ❏ Update passport or any travel documents for honeymoon.
- ❏ Make bachelorette and bachelor party reservations.
- ❏ Finalize hotel room blocks.
- ❏ Book morning-after brunch at the hotel.
- ❏ Have a spa day!

6 months

- ❏ Order invitations and buy postage.
- ❏ Make wedding dress alteration appointments.
- ❏ Book rehearsal with your venue or church.
- ❏ Finalize choices of tablecloth colors, centerpieces, signage, and favors.
- ❏ Ask the caterer for a tasting date.
- ❏ Set up a venue visit if you have questions.
- ❏ Investigate what to do if you are changing your name.
- ❏ Start a wedding registry.
- ❏ Start to formulate your wedding day timeline.

❐ If you receive gifts, write thank you notes.

❐ Have a massage or facial day!

3 months

❐ Send invitations.

❐ Have a system in place for receiving RSVPs.

❐ Finalize menu and flowers.

❐ Ask DJ for forms for music choices, if not already received.

❐ Ask your photographer for any forms they require.

❐ Attend your wedding shower.

❐ Purchase thank you gifts for family and friends.

❐ Plan favors and welcome bags.

❐ Start writing your vows.

❐ Make mani/pedi appointments.

❐ Take a yoga or other relaxing class.

1-2 months

❐ Have fun at your bachelorette party.

❐ Apply for your marriage license.

❐ Pick up your dress from alterations.

❐ Make a seating chart.

❐ Do a final walkthrough at your venue.

❐ Confirm rehearsal dinner location and time.

❐ Invite your bridal party and any others to your rehearsal and dinner.

❐ Make a list of photos you want with family and friends.

❐ Have a day off where you do whatever you want!

2 Weeks

☐ Give the final guest count to your venue and caterer.

☐ Finalize floor plan with venue.

☐ Confirm the arrival times of your vendors.

☐ Assemble checks and tips for vendors.

☐ Write your partner their day-of wedding note.

☐ Practice your vows.

☐ Start packing a bag for your wedding night and/or honeymoon.

☐ Send your final day-of wedding timeline to your venue and vendors.

☐ Give your vendors a contact person(s) for the wedding day.

☐ Decide who you want in the first one or two rows at your ceremony.

☐ Spend time in nature. Take a walk or visit a botanic garden.

The Day Before

☐ Eat a healthy meal. Drink plenty of water.

☐ Give the marriage certificate to your officiant at rehearsal.

☐ Drop off anything to your church or venue that you possibly can.

☐ Give your wedding bands to your pastor or a trusted friend.

☐ Try to get a good night's sleep! Calm any jitters with deep breathing and affirmations.

Notes

_____

_____

_____

_____

_____

_____

_____

_____

_____

_____

_____

_____

_____

_____

_____

_____

_____

_____

_____

THE MINDFUL BRIDE

THE "B" WORD (BUDGET!) OR FINANCIAL WEDDING SUCCESS

*A solid budget is the cornerstone
of good wedding planning.*

In my years as a wedding coordinator, I've met many couples who were financially savvy. They recognized their limitations, set boundaries for spending, and adhered to a budget. These were the calm ones, smiling and happy on their wedding day.

On the flip side, I've also worked with couples who overshot their budgets and didn't always live in reality. I could see the stress in their faces as they got closer to their wedding day.

I define financial wedding success as the ability to comfortably pay for all the commitments of your day. The best way for The Mindful Bride to achieve this comes down to one word — honesty. This involves a heart-to-heart reckoning regarding "what can I truly afford?"

Write down a budget amount that you can live with. Be honest with yourself. The budget should be one that enables you and your fiancé to sleep at night and that you won't be paying off for years to come.

Once you have decided on an amount, I advise getting it out of your head and onto your computer or a piece of paper. You may wish to create an online master file for all your wedding information (I like Google Sheets or Excel spreadsheets) with multiple tabs. Use the tabs for whatever you want — budget, vendors, bridal party, and even guest RSVP's. If you prefer writing things down, get yourself a nice wedding planner book. You might also want a multi-pocket file for storing contracts.

On your first tab of your spreadsheet, begin listing the things that could be expenses towards your wedding day.

Here's a good checklist. Add only what pertains to your day.

Wedding Essentials
❐ Wedding Bands
❐ Wedding License
❐ Wedding Insurance
❐ Officiant
❐ Invitations & Postage

Clothing & Accessories
❐ Shower Dress
❐ Wedding Dress
❐ Reception Dress (your call)
❐ Shoes & Handbag & Jewelry

Venue Related
❐ Caterer
❐ Rentals (linens, tents, dishware, flatware)
❐ Bartenders
❐ Alcohol

Vendors
- ❐ Wedding Planner or Day-of Wedding Coordinator
- ❐ Hair and Makeup
- ❐ Transportation (limo and/or shuttle)
- ❐ Florist
- ❐ Photographer & Videographer
- ❐ DJ/ Entertainment
- ❐ Pet Care
- ❐ Child Care

Extras
- ❐ Bridal Party Gifts
- ❐ Church Fees
- ❐ Extra Decor Items
- ❐ Tips

I could list expenditures for these various vendors, but the truth is, you will find these professionals in all different price ranges. And much of this pricing is dependent on the area in which you live, and the market for that area.

For most of my career, I've been a *"day-of wedding"* coordinator. Many of my couples find me when they've made most of their major vendor decisions. If they do bring me on board early, even before they choose their venue, I ask them for their preferences, their budget, and how much time they will have to invest in their planning. The reason for this is many venue options involve multiple decisions and separate contracts, so they automatically create more work.

When I see a venue that requires renting everything (even tables and chairs), this raises my internal red flag. These venues typically also have a select group of caterers or even just one exclusive caterer. In some instances, they even dictate the rental companies you must choose from for linens, lighting, stage, dance floor, and other add-ons.

This type of venue may also be managed by a non-profit organization that raises money by renting their facilities; however, they are not typically full-time wedding/event venues. Sometimes they have stricter rules that both the wedding party and guests must abide by. The result may be a higher *overall* cost because many wedding day necessities are not included in the venue's base price.

Over the years, I've seen couples sign up for things they struggle to pay for after the wedding. Initial visits to wedding venues can be a heady experience. Being with your loved one as you gaze at an outdoor barn, a botanic garden, or a gorgeous hotel can be especially emotional. You envision yourself there and think, *"this is perfect, exactly what I want."*

Oftentimes your well-planned budget may allow for a $5000 venue cost. But realistically, that could be easily exceeded if you don't dig a bit deeper. Check all caterers on the preferred catering list before you sign and know what is included (tables, chairs, linens, etc.) and what is not. Calculate these details alongside your estimated guest number to achieve a more realistic budget without surprises.

You *can* do a beautiful non-profit, botanic garden, or hotel wedding if you investigate all the costs ahead of time and know you can afford it (remember to make sure that you don't need a $4000 tent for the caterer to grill food under, for example).

ProTip: *One more thing I want you to consider relates to monetary gifts from your wedding day. It is unwise to rely* *on the money or checks that you receive on your wedding day to pay your expenses. Use that money for something you mutually decide on: a vacation, furniture, or even the beginning of your future down payment on a house.*

To summarize, a solid budget is the foundation of planning a wedding. Be realistic. Look at all your costs during the planning process and don't just dive in with the thought that you'll figure it out later.

Notes

VENDORS
& SERVICES

*A good vendor will do everything in their power
to make your day fabulous.*

If you decide to have a full wedding day with all the bells and whistles, your vendor selections can make the difference between an amazing experience or an unhappy one. You can do several things to find quality vendors.

- Ask recently married friends for referrals.
- Get their contact information if you go to a wedding and like the vendors.
- Join a local wedding group on social media and ask other couples who they've used.
- Do searches and send emails to vendors, asking for packages and pricing.
- Read all <u>recent</u> reviews you can find on the vendors that are of interest.

ProTip: *If a vendor has many good reviews with a singular bad one, this is usually due to a difficult client ... and not the vendor.*

It is always advisable to sign a contract before any money is exchanged. This is to protect you. Read over all contracts carefully and ask questions if there is something you don't understand. No vendor should ask for all cash; most will want an initial deposit, then a final payment a month or so before your wedding. Get a receipt (in writing) of your deposit when you make the payment. Trust your gut. If any vendor gives you a line about cash payments and no contract, move on. Immediately.

Venue

I'll start with venues because I consider this to be one of the most important decisions you'll make. Think about whether you want everything in one place — catering staff, rooms for guests, full bar, on-site parking — or do you want to piece together many different parts to make a collective whole?

If you have your wedding at a hotel, the venue will have a full service banquet staff. Everything will likely be included – tablecloths, linen napkins, silverware, dishes, waitstaff, etc. — at one price. They may even offer centerpieces as part of their offer. If you request a room block for your guests, a good hotel may also extend a complimentary suite for a restful pre-wedding night and for your hair and make-up on the wedding day!

Non-profit spaces are desirable these days and can include park buildings, museums, or landmarks. As I mentioned in the budget chapter, remember that you may have to rent everything, even tables and chairs. These are the weddings that seem innocently inexpensive at first, until you put all the numbers down and realize they aren't cheap. Live in reality.

Be realistic about what you can afford, and ask detailed questions.

Barns or outdoor venues (sometimes these are also non-profits) may have tables, chairs, gazebos, and other amenities. These spaces are offering more and more features due to growing competition. One thing I must insist on: make sure they have bathrooms with flushing toilets. Dismiss a venue that requires you to rent Porta Johns or bathroom trailers!

Questions to ask your potential venue:

- Will there be a day-of event coordinator on site at your wedding, and if so, what are their responsibilities? Ask for a list!
- Can you provide a copy of your current contract?
- How much does the venue carry in liability coverage, and does it include alcohol liability?
- What are the payment terms?
- Who will be my primary contact if I have questions along the way?
- What is specifically provided for my wedding regarding tables, chairs, linens, plates, and staffing?
- How many visits am I allowed between the date I sign the contract, and the day of my wedding? Will a coordinator be present to answer my questions?
- How can I accommodate any handicapped individuals? Are there parking spaces, ramps, elevators, and handicapped accessible bathrooms?
- What are my responsibilities to the venue — clean up that night, extra insurance?

Photographers and Videographers

Photographers often have their own style. Look at their website photos carefully for a look and feel that resonates with your own. Ask for pricing and consider packaging your engagement and wedding photos together. You can use the engagement photos for a "Save the Date" announcement. Send it around the holidays and you have your Christmas card!

An experienced wedding photographer will work together with you to create a collection of images you'll cherish for the rest of your life. Some photographers also have their own videographer team, so ask about this as well. A videographer can film your ceremony and reception or both. If this is important to you, look at multiple vendors, their wedding videos, and see what you like.

Questions for your potential photographer:

- How long have you been a professional photographer?
- Do you carry liability insurance?
- Will you bring a second shooter?
- Do you have a videographer on your team?
- What are the tiered costs for coming to the hotel or wherever hair/makeup will be done, plus ceremony, plus reception?
- Have you photographed at this venue and/or religious institution before?
- What attire do you wear on wedding day?
- What are the terms for payment?
- Can you provide a sample copy of your contract?

Caterer

Hiring the right caterer will make your planning process much easier. Food is a big expense and this is one area that people often talk about afterwards! Take notice of how long it takes for a caterer to respond to your emails. If they take longer than a day or two, that is probably how they are going to communicate going forward. If this won't drive you crazy that's fine ... but the number one complaint I hear about caterers is their lack of communication. Whenever possible, find one who responds within two business days. *Remember that the end of the week tends to be busier for caterers because the bulk of their work is on weekends, so adjust your expectations accordingly.*

Read online reviews and request menus and pricing. See if you can do a tasting before you hire them. This doesn't always happen but if you are lucky, you might be invited to an event or wedding where you can taste a caterer's food beforehand.

If you choose an outdoor/barn/park type venue, it is likely there will be a select list of caterers to choose from. Proceed carefully and investigate each one. Ask for a sample invoice for everything you'll need including any rentals like tents, chafers, dishes, etc.

Think about your preference. Is it a buffet or sit-down dinner? A buffet is usually less expensive because it requires less wait staff. You can also offer guests multiple entrees — chicken, beef, even seafood — which satisfies a broader range of tastes. There is truly no negative side to a buffet unless you personally prefer one style to the other.

For a sit-down dinner, guests will need to choose a main entrée from your menu. There should also be a vegetarian option, a gluten-free option, and a vegan option. These options should be noted on your RSVP card, or on your wedding website.

Also, for a sit-down dinner, a good caterer will provide you with a spreadsheet where you will note each guest table and what meals will be served at that table. For example: table three might have eight guests with three chicken, three beef, and two gluten-free meals (yes, it should be that organized!) Furthermore, you can also create guest place cards which denote, with a small letter or sticker, what each guest is getting. (Isn't a buffet sounding easier?)

Please also remember to include your vendors in your final meal number. This is a standard procedure, and it is good to ask caterers up front if there is a reduced charge or any special consideration for vendors. Also ask the venue if there is a spot where vendors eat, unless you'd be ok with having a table at your reception especially for vendors. This is always a nice gesture, and I can't tell you what it means to a vendor to eat the same meal as the guests and to sit at a table inside the same reception area.

Non-profit venues may or may not have alcohol service. If you provide your own alcohol, see if you can return unopened, unused bottles to your source. Chances are your Uncle Joe or Cousin Suzanne will not be allowed to bartend. Your caterer may offer RAMP (Responsible Alcohol Management Program) certified bartenders and have the liability insurance to back this up. Or you may need to hire professional bartenders. Ask your caterer if they provide alcohol service, and what exactly is provided — ice, cups, napkins, etc.

Whatever caterer you choose, make sure they are *full*

*service caterer*s. Do not be tempted by drop-off catering. I know drop-off will cost less, but you will need wait staff to stay until the end to bus tables and even help clean up your venue. Don't expect your guests to clean up after themselves. They shouldn't have to ... and won't do so.

Questions for your potential caterers:

- Are you a full service caterer with your own wait staff? Can you stay until the end of the reception and help clean up?
- Can you provide proof of liability insurance? (if they are on a list of preferred caterers, the venue will ask this of them)
- Do you provide alcohol service, including RAMP certified bartenders? What other items can you provide for bar service, if so? (optional, based on venue)
- Please provide a full sample invoice, including any rentals such as plates, silverware, tents, linens, etc.
- Please provide your menus, including costs.
- Can you accommodate gluten-free, nut-free, dairy-free, or any specific choices?
- When can I schedule a tasting?

Florist

You can spend a fortune, or very little on flowers. Some of my brides have opted for silks or even paper flower bouquets, which look surprisingly wonderful. And I love a good bling bouquet made with sparkly, new or vintage pins.

Centerpieces with fresh flowers can be expensive so

shop around for pricing if this is what you want. If you go with seasonal flowers, your total cost could be less. Tulips for spring, hydrangeas for summer, and sunflowers in late summer or early fall are examples of seasonal flowers. Be careful about getting flowers that have strong smells. Some guests may sneeze or have asthma, and perfumy flowers like lilies can trigger runny noses and watery eyes.

If you decide to make your own live flower bouquets and centerpieces, watch videos and don't wait until the last minute to put them together. Especially if you are using fresh flowers, you must have a solid plan in place for ordering, picking up, designing, and storing until your wedding day. You may have to order flowers a few months in advance, so investigate sources and don't cut it too close to your wedding date. If you do order fresh flowers, remember that upon delivery, you will need to get them into water as soon as they arrive, so multiple buckets are going to be needed. If you make bouquets or boutonnieres, you will need refrigerator space for them. Also think about transport. If you make fresh centerpieces, how and when will you get them to (and from) the venue?

ProTip: *If you deliver your flowers to the venue the day before your wedding, make sure the room they are stored in has heat or A/C, depending on the time of year. If you refrigerate them at the venue, be sure they are in the fridge and <u>not</u> the freezer. This happened to us once! The family could not tell the difference between the stainless steel fridge and the refrigerator so, unfortunately, they put some mason jars of flowers into the freezer the night before the wedding! Two hours before the reception my assistants were placing* *batches of fresh flowers in new mason jars, because the other floral centerpieces were frozen solid!*

Questions for your potential florist:

- What types of floral bouquets and centerpieces do you recommend for my time of year?
- Will you deliver to the hotel the morning of the wedding as well as the venue if necessary?
- Can you provide a cost in advance for the bouquets and any else I choose?
- Do you have a contract, or will you provide terms in writing?
- Do you offer choices if substitutions are necessary?
- Does your service include pinning boutonnieres and handing out bouquets?

Bakery

The big multi-tiered wedding cakes of the past seem less popular these days, replaced by simple cakes that a couple can easily use for ceremonial cake cutting. Many of my couples opt for this and then order sheet cakes for the guests' portions. They save their own smaller cake, or they share it with their families. I strongly advise couples to order two thirds their guest count in cake because (honestly) many people will not eat dessert. Instruct your caterer to place slices on a dessert or coffee station so guests have the option. Or ask if cake can be taken around to the tables and guests again, given the option. Don't waste cake by having a slice placed at every place setting. If you are having other dessert options — a cookie table, a variety of cake slices or cupcakes — you can comfortably cut back on your cake count.

Questions for your bakery:

- What type of wedding desserts do you provide — cupcakes, cookies, tiered cake, or other options?
- Can you provide a price list for everything?
- What is your delivery charge?
- Who will be my main point of contact within the bakery?
- When do I need to make my final choices?
- What are the terms of payment?
- Can you supply guest *take-home* boxes for cake or cookies?

Pet Care

Pet care at weddings is becoming more and more popular. Unless your venue is super accommodating to animals, it pays to have a dog handler for your pooch. This type of service will take care of your dog leading up to your ceremony and likely take them home, or a designated place, afterwards.

The flip side of this is having your dog(s) at the wedding, leaving them there for the whole evening, and having family or friends lined up to watch them. This also entails cleaning up after them as no venue will be pleased at having to do this during the reception or afterwards. Nor do you want guests stepping in fresh poo with their blingy pumps. The Mindful Bride is thoughtful to the venue and courteous to guests. It is good etiquette to take care of your pets yourself and not depend on others.

ProTip: *Have your dog at your ceremony, and for photography afterwards, then have someone take them home. It's really not a fun evening for a dog.*

Questions for a potential pet care service:
- What are your qualifications?
- Do you carry liability insurance?
- Can you provide a sample copy of your contract?
- Will there be two doggy caregivers on my wedding day? One to handle my dog, and one for any clean up necessary?
- What do you provide and what do you expect me to provide, including poo bags, leash, treats, etc.?

Childcare

Most weddings today are adult affairs. This can be tricky when you invite out-of-town guests with small children. If you really want them to be there, think about offering childcare.

The easiest scenario in this case is to have a hotel wedding and pay a professionally licensed sitter or sitters who will watch and entertain the children. This is not an easy job, but these individuals are experienced and usually bring toys and games for the children to play with, based on their age. You can even ask the hotel if there is an empty conference room on the wedding day that the children and sitters can occupy. Have kid-friendly food delivered there, and snacks and drinks available. A couple of tables with board games and coloring books and crayons is helpful. Don't have crafts with glue and glitter. Later in the evening, they can go up to the hotel rooms for a movie or to be tucked in.

This is the kindest option if you want out-of-town friends and families with young children to be able to participate in your wedding weekend.

Questions for Child Care providers:

- What are your qualifications?
- Can you provide state clearances for the workers who will be caring for the children on that day? (Have someone match up these clearances to the actual workers on wedding day.)
- Can you provide references?
- Do you carry liability insurance?
- Do you have a contract and/or terms of service?

DJ/Band/Lighting

I have included lighting with the DJ category because most bands or DJs will provide lighting for a small extra cost. This is worth it because it adds spots of color throughout your reception areas. As for a DJ or band, it's whatever you can afford. Many DJs are great at playing a variety of music, getting people to dance, and keeping the evening going. Bands are also great at this as well. So, it depends on your personal preference and what you'd really like.

One additional thought: make sure your band or DJ will do the announcements at the reception. This includes the entry of the bridal party and any other announcements during the evening, such as the cake cutting, first dance, etc. All good DJs are professional announcers so don't hesitate to ask about this important role when you interview them.

Questions to ask a potential DJ:

- Are you an experienced DJ?
- What are your qualifications?
- Do you carry liability insurance?

- Can you provide references or reviews?
- Do you provide a contract?
- What are your terms?
- Are you experienced at making announcements?
- What type of paperwork will I need to fill out regarding my choices of music?
- Are you willing to add special requests at the wedding reception?
- How far ahead of cocktail hour and reception do you arrive?
- If the events of the evening are in different rooms, do you have multiple speakers to be able to accommodate this?
- Do you provide lighting and, if you've been at this venue, what are your recommendations?

ProTip: *I'd ask any vendor who will be on site during your ceremony and/or reception what they typically wear on wedding days. I've seen photographers show up in purple shorts, jeans, khakis, and other oh-too-casual attire. If your wedding is super laid back and this won't bother you, that's fine. But if you are having a dressy affair, I'd ask what they typically wear. I once did a black tie wedding where the father of the bride insisted that he did not want any videographer showing up in cargo shorts! He wanted every vendor dressed appropriately. I sent an email a month in advance of the wedding, basically informing all vendors that the expectation of the family was that everyone would be professionally dressed. It worked. Everyone showed up looking great and the father was very pleased!*

Invitations

Most invitations these days are printed by couples themselves or ordered online. Stationary stores are rare but still exist and they often have books of invitations for you to pick from. Approximately one half of my couples do a standard RSVP card, and the other half use a wedding website.

I favor an RSVP card because I think this is easier for people to do, rather than get the invite, type a website address in their browser search bar, and figure out how to RSVP. This is especially difficult for older adults who are not always internet-savvy. Think about your guest list and what's easiest for all.

What to look for regarding wedding invitations:

- Cheap is not necessarily good. If you can order paper and printing samples, go for it. Do this at least six months in advance of your wedding so that you can see what you will receive.
- Is there an accompanying website to your invitation site, where guests can RSVP?
- Can you order everything from one spot — "Save the Dates", invitations, RSVP cards, and thank you notes?
- Sign up for email newsletters for discount or coupon codes!
- If you are unhappy with your finished products, is there a solid return/refund policy?

ProTip: *I have a code for Minted.com that will save you 35% off Save the Dates, and 25% off other wedding stationary! It is:* **WEDPLKATHERINESDAUGHTER**

Day-of Coordinator or Wedding Planner

As you can imagine, I am partial to this category because I am a *Day-of Wedding* coordinator. There is a difference between a coordinator and a planner. A planner will help you make decisions on theme, decor, and vendors ... and will generally involve themselves in the entire planning process. A coordinator usually comes on board a month or two in advance and is mainly focused on the logistics of the day. Both will make sure your wishes are carried out and go according to plan. They should also help you create a timeline for your day if you do not have one already. Planners are more expensive than coordinators because they do much more. I do believe that every wedding should have at least one coordinator so that the couple and their families can fully enjoy their day without worry.

Planners/coordinators will also take care of any last-minute glitches. Yes, they happen! I had a bakery call me once to say that the three tired, three layered white wedding cake with raspberry filling began leaning while on the way to the venue. They ended up driving back to the bakery to fix it and did so by eliminating one of the tiers. The bride would have never known, except her sister spilled the beans later! But truly, we have solved many last minute mishaps and the bride, groom, and their families never find out!

Many venues require all decor, gifts, props, and alcohol to be out by an hour or two after the end of a wedding. This is especially true at park and non-profit venues. A good exit plan is a must, and a venue or independent coordinator can assist with this process.

**Questions to ask your potential
Day-of Wedding Coordinator:**

- Do you have a list of the services you provide?
- How far in advance of my wedding day do you come on board?
- Can you go with me for a final walk through at my venue? (typically, 3-4 weeks before your wedding date)
- How early do you show up on wedding day?
- Do you stay until the end of my wedding day and help pack up?
- Do you work with any vendors, or do you only work with specific vendors?
- Do you contact vendors before the wedding day to line up arrival times?

To summarize, the vendors you choose should have great reviews, communicate promptly, address concerns, and be able to provide a list of services and a contract. They should be dressed professionally and work together to give you the spectacular wedding day you envision!

Notes

_____
_____
_____
_____
_____
_____
_____
_____
_____
_____
_____
_____
_____
_____
_____
_____
_____
_____
_____
_____
_____
_____
_____

YOUR BRIDAL PARTY

*A good bridal party helps ensure a bride
feels celebrated, loved, and surrounded by joy
throughout the entire wedding journey.*

Weddings can make or break friendships. This is why the choices you make regarding your bridal party are so very important. I've known brides with unrealistic expectations; they were disappointed with their bridal party's actions yet failed to communicate their wishes. These are the brides who ended up doing everything themselves ... and resenting it. On the wedding day, I could feel their tension; it showed up in terse comments and silence.

What kind of person are you when it comes to friendships? Maybe you have many friends or just a select few. Do you have a large or small immediate family? When it comes to your bridal party, choose wisely and with careful thought and consideration. Your attendants can and often will impact your peace of mind in the coming months.

The reasons for having a bridal party are twofold: including cherished friends in your big day is most important, followed by having trusted resources by your side for support up to and on your wedding day. A bride must be willing to give up some degree of control if assistance is desired. Make a list of your potential bridesmaids and consider their personalities.

Then, answer the following questions:
- Do they know each other?
- Do you think they'll communicate well with each other?
- Will they work together as a team?
- What are their financial situations?

If they know and like each other, that's a bonus. If they don't know each other, do you think their personalities will mesh well, or could there be friction? Which ones answer most quickly when you text, call, or email? Who steps up to the plate and proactively looks for solutions, or knows how to problem solve? Who likes to work alone, and who likes to be part of a team? It is important to have a leader (usually the Maid of Honor, but not always), but you also need worker bees.

Being a bridesmaid can be quite a financial commitment. In addition to paying for their dress and shoes, the bridesmaids of today are often expected to help with shower expenses. Some will plan and all will contribute financially if there's a bachelorette weekend.

Ask yourself if each bridesmaid you are considering can afford to serve this important role. If someone you sincerely want is in college, on a strict budget, or financially challenged, will you, or someone in their family, be willing to help them? You both may need to have a confidential conversation to gauge their true feelings. If they want to be a bridesmaid and are willing to accept help, assist them confidentially and without expectation of return favors.

ProTip: *Assisting someone financially is a great token of love and compassion. When brides provide this assistance, it* *should be offered with no-strings-attached. Maintaining this attitude will keep resentments at bay and friendships intact.*

Next, ask yourself these questions:

- What are my expectations for my bridal party?
- Who am I asking out of obligation vs. from a point of friendship? In other words, do you really want your third cousin, or do you feel obligated to make the offer?
- If there are several bridesmaids who are unable to help much due to their location or work situations, will I be okay with that?
- What kind of communicator am I?
  - I can list my bridal party's duties in advance, designate jobs based on personalities and skill sets, and communicate these responsibilities verbally at first, then summarized in follow-up emails.
  - I can communicate throughout my planning process in a mature way, addressing issues if they come up.
  - I can be understanding of friends who may decline my offer, as they may not have the money or time to invest.

ProTip: *Don't invite friends or family to your bridal party out of a sense of obligation. Invite who you want. Unless you truly want to get to know someone better, or don't want to create a difficult family dynamic, it's better to skip someone you barely know, or are not sure you will get along with.*

Determining price ranges for a dress, shoes, hair, makeup, and any other financial expectations *in advance* is helpful information to share with your potential bridesmaids. There are plenty of gorgeous wedding websites with reasonably priced bridal attire. Shoe choices can be up to an individual and no longer must be identical. Dresses do not need to be "matchy-matchy!" I worked with a wonderful bride who let her six bridesmaids choose whatever long dress they wanted. They made personalized choices, and the result was a beautiful wedding party!

Within your bridal party, the most valuable choice you will make is the naming of your Maid of Honor (MOH). This is the person who can unite the rest of the bridal party, keep the spirit of the wedding going, and be your biggest cheerleader.

In choosing your MOH, think of the following:

- Is this a person I can comfortably share my feelings with, good and bad? Will they keep my confidence (seriously, there are people who cannot keep secrets) if I ask them to?
- Are they dependable?
- Are they a good communicator and team player?
- Do they have the financial resources needed for all responsibilities?
- Are they mature and able to handle conflict in a positive way?

You can see where I'm going with this. Your MOH will set the tone for the rest of the bridal party. If your MOH is your sister, cousin or other family member and lives in another state or is too busy, then someone else in your wedding party will need to step in to fill those shoes.

Choose wisely and thoughtfully — doing so will save you many headaches and create the bridal party dream team that you desire. The likelihood of misunderstandings will also be minimized if your expectations are clearly communicated and agreed upon in advance. Another pathway to being The Mindful Bride!

One more option I want to mention is *not* having a bridal party. I've worked with brides who made this decision. Even so, most still had a maid of honor and a best man, but that's it. After much consideration, these brides recognized that they did not want a lot of hoopla around their day, nor did they want to impose the financial obligation on anyone. They chose to keep it simple, and everything was fine!

Ring Bearers and Flower Girls

Nothing is more adorable than a ring bearer holding a white pillow with rings, or a flower girl or two holding a basket filled with rose petals. If you are blessed to have young ones in the family, add them to your bridal party. If the parents of the children are also in the bridal party, this is the best-case scenario; they will be at rehearsal and be of great assistance when it comes time to walk down the aisle. If the children are little, parents will often hold their hand as they walk down the aisle. It's beautiful to see.

Children under the age of four should not walk down the aisle alone. I've seen young ones do fine at rehearsal, then on the wedding day, they melt into a pile of tears in the back of the church. Think of the pressure of walking alone in front of all those guests! Recruit an older child to walk with a younger one unless one or both parents are in the bridal party.

ProTip: *At ceremony time, ring bearers should not be given the real wedding bands. Those should be entrusted to the officiant/priest or the best man. Use fake bands to tie to your ring bearer's pillow.*

To summarize, choose your bridal party wisely. It is very important to select friends and family who will work together on your behalf to form your dream team! It is your responsibility to communicate your wishes to your bridesmaids, and to show appreciation for their willingness to be a part of your wedding day.

Notes

CELEBRATION
& COMPROMISE

When family matters meet wedding dreams,
aim to keep joy in the journey.

Family Members. Can't live with them, can't live without them. If you are lucky enough to have wonderful parents and future in-laws, you are blessed. Oftentimes, weddings can bring out the worst behavior in even the most mature of adults.

Imagine a groom's grandparents upsetting a family by saying they won't come. They do show up but proceed to sit in the front in the pew that was intended for the bride's parents. Picture future in-laws who pull their financial assistance because a couple made choices they disagreed with. The in-laws did not attend the wedding and influenced other family members to not attend as well (their loss, as the wedding was gorgeous!).

At one rehearsal, I found out there might be an interruption to the wedding ceremony by an old boyfriend, and bouncers would be stationed in the back of the church by the entrance doors (nothing happened, whew!).

Challenging circumstances creep up in every celebration so don't be surprised if one or two pop up during your planning time. The key is not to be overcome with negativity, anxiety, or despondency. *There is always a solution for The*

Mindful Bride. From handling bossy parents to guilt inducing grandmas, here's some tried and true advice.

Family Conflicts

Most conflicts are between parents and the marrying couple. If either or both sets of the parents are contributing to the wedding, there are likely to be statements like, *"I want it this way and that's that."* Or there are endless conversations where no one wants to back down. I've witnessed this personally on video chats. Often the biggest sources of conflict are whether to get married in a church or not, the option of a buffet or sit-down dinner, and the choice of a rustic or traditional venue. The list goes on and on.

Bottom line is, *how important is it?* If you can't sleep or are having massive arguments with parents over minute decisions, someone will have to let go. Decide exactly how important an issue it is, and whether it's worth pushing your point. If you need a neutral party to settle an issue, this is where clergy, or a wedding planner/coordinator, can draw the battle lines and bring everyone to their senses.

ProTip: *Don't hesitate to bring a trusted individual into the fold. Choose someone who is calm, patient, and a good problem solver.*

Regarding financial situations with parents or other family members, here is the best case scenario: if parents are paying for all or even some of the wedding, I suggest the couple open a wedding checking account and deposit any monies that are given to them. When the amount of money is first discussed or given, *that is the perfect time* to ask if there are any expectations about any wedding components including guest/invitation list, menu, venue, or anything else that could be a potential source of conflict.

If criteria are presented, write the details down in front of the family member and acknowledge or discuss it. The Mindful Bride must respect these types of agreements. A lack of integrity or denial regarding previous agreements will sow much unhappiness.

If there are no criteria, I would also acknowledge this. It would help if there was someone present as a witness, your fiancé or one of your bridesmaids for example, unless you truly trust the individual. People occasionally have memory lapses and remember something different than what was discussed. Sometimes this is intentional, but almost always they simply forget what was said.

ProTip: *You are allowed to change your mind. If you have a prior agreement with someone, be up front and honest with that person if you have a change of heart. Openly discuss your second thoughts, and you will likely get a stamp of approval.*

The special checking account is the easiest way to handle deposits and transactions — a parent or family member can contribute to the wedding funds, and the couple can distribute funds to their vendors. If you have an overspending tendency, be sure to enlist someone who can help you stay in check and on budget. Accountability is hard, but even harder is asking for more money the month before your wedding.

The other scenario is when parents investigate vendors, negotiate contracts, and pay invoices themselves. This happens when mom and/or dad are doing the bulk of the wedding planning, especially if the marrying couple is busy with work obligations.

Family members often pressure a couple regarding guest lists, menu, decor, anything and everything! The younger the couple (early 20's), and the more the family is contributing, the more I see this happen. Older couples (30's+), who are usually more financially established, are less likely to cave to family pressures. Even if they are receiving help financially, older couples are more likely to stick to their ideas.

For example, if a family member wants to pay for your florist but then dictates what types of flowers you choose, decide if those flowers are what you really want. If you don't like their ideas, please don't settle and be unhappy about your floral choices forever. Meet your relative in person and explain what you want to do. Accept any differences gracefully. Say thank you, no matter which way you go. If you have your own ideas, and have the funds to pay for it, stick to your own wishes and get what you want.

ProTip: *Don't let family issues fester and aggravate you. If there is a disagreement at any point, stay calm and reach out. Make a coffee or lunch date. In a day or two people will usually come to their senses, and a rational conversation can begin. Issues are more easily resolved early on, rather than when weeks or months pass by.*

Bride and Fiancé Compromises

Opposites attract, remember? If you and your fiancé

thought the same about everything, think how boring life would be! There's a good chance that, if your future spouse is involved in the planning, there are bound to be differences. Decide early on how you will make decisions. Make compromises where and when needed.

If your fiancé wants to be involved in some of the wedding decisions, embrace that desire at an early point in your planning. Discuss your budget and decide on colors, theme, venue ideas ... you name it. Talk about each category separately. Draw selections from a hat if there is conflict. The Mindful Bride doesn't harbor resentments if everything doesn't go their way. You'll win some battles, and lose some. You'll compromise. That's also the makings of a good marriage!

Nosy family members

Let's say you decide to take a year or more for your engagement and subsequent wedding planning. Your Grandma Marie is wondering why and gives you an earful when you bump into her at the family reunion. *"Whaddaya mean a year! Heck, I got married in three months after my engagement!"* Here are some comebacks for people who ask you why your wedding is a year or more away.

- "Weddings are expensive these days and we need time to save up."
- "Would you like to start a Go Fund Me for our wedding?" (make sure you smile and chuckle when you say this!)
- "We are in no hurry and want to take our time planning."

Then, as my husband calls it, pull a "Jo" (that's my nickname) and CHANGE THE SUBJECT. It's none of their business but if you don't want to appear rude, then say, *"How's your sister Kate, brother Lou, blah blah blah?"* and soon they will be off in a different direction, completely on another page of conversation. People love to talk about themselves!

Please remember this. If you accept money from anyone, you should send a personal thank you note now, and then again after the wedding. It's nice to mention what you'll use the funds for, or what you will be purchasing with that monetary gift.

The delicate dance of family and wedding decisions need not result in a *be all, end all.* In other words, it's not definitive. Think of it like a beautiful waltz, where the music plays as you gracefully dance between each of your loved ones, turning and weaving as you go, confidently in charge of your own moves.

Notes

CRAFTING YOUR WEDDING VISION

Choosing the perfect decor to set the scene
and transform your wedding vision into reality.

You've set your budget, hired your vendors, and are well on your way to planning your wedding day. Chances are you already have a Pinterest board or other styling ideas! Colors, font types, and themes are emerging within your vision. This is the time to nail down your thoughts about decor.

For the church or ceremony, decor can include pew accents, "unplugged" signage (asking guests not to use phones or take pictures during the ceremony), candles, programs, and florals. Reception embellishments can be table numbers and florals, favors, and other special flourishes.

Let's start with two types of ceremonies: the church ceremony and the venue ceremony.

Church Ceremony

Church ceremonies can be as minimal or embellished as you wish. The place to start is with the rules. When you book your ceremony, ask what you are and are not allowed to do. Some churches do not want the flower girls to throw real petals. Others have said no to the traditional "crash," the white runway that is unfolded for the bride to walk down, due to tripping concerns. Some churches do not allow rice but will allow bubbles or bird seed. (I favor bubbles as they do not get in anyone's hair!) Here's a checklist to run by your officiant.

- ❒ Roses for the mothers, or a candle for them to light together?
- ❒ Pew bows or other decor such as ribbons to mark off the family seating
- ❒ Altar flowers
- ❒ Ceremony programs (ask if they have any kind of template)
- ❒ Rice or bubbles when the couple exits
- ❒ Crash, if you want one
- ❒ Any signage you are considering with "welcome to the wedding of" and/or "unplugged" messaging

Venue Ceremony

Many venues have areas for ceremonies. Some are outdoor, others are indoor. Again, the first thing to ask about is the rules. The checklist for the church ceremony is applicable here, but I would also ask about the following, if you are interested.

- ❒ Embellishing an archway or gazebo in silk or fresh flowers
- ❒ Signage upon entering the area and, if so, do they have strong easels
- ❒ Vases or baskets of flowers
- ❒ Umbrellas for guests
- ❒ Candles in protective glass cylinders (to protect table linens from wax)
- ❒ Tents to cover guests in case of extreme heat or rain

If you want an outdoor ceremony, consider what the weather could be. If it will be chilly, you may want to have baskets of rolled up blankets available. If it might rain or be excessively hot, umbrellas or handheld fans are a nice touch.

ProTip: *Avoid using large mirrors for signage outdoors. If they fall, you can imagine the scene! Use lightweight chalkboards or poster boards and secure them to the easel if it's a windy day.*

Reception (Table Decor and Signage)

What do you want your reception room to look like when you and your guests walk through the door? What is your vision? Let's break it down into two main components: Table Decor and Signage.

Table decor options can include:
- Table Size: round or rectangle?
- Tablecloths: short or to the floor, and what color?
- Centerpieces: fresh or silk flowers, or non-floral options?
- Favors: at each guest setting or at the sign-in table?
- Special Tables: sweetheart table, bridal party table, memory tables, dessert tables, etc.

If you are having a buffet dinner, the napkins and silverware will be at each place setting, and the dinner plates will be at the start of the buffet. If you are having a sit-down dinner, the same place setting will apply, and the caterer will bring the dinner plates to each guest. Remember we discussed having a full service caterer vs. drop off catering? The caterer will have their waitstaff do the place settings, and many of them will lay the tablecloths as well.

Unless you are having a very casual wedding, most wedding tablecloths flow *to the floor*. It is more elegant and eye pleasing. Centerpieces can be anything from fresh flowers to books and teacups with plants. Many options exist and can be tailored to you and your fiancé's tastes or hobbies. Having small, framed pictures of your travels together or other moments in time personalizes the wedding and makes it more of your own.

As far as favors go, there are lots of choices. A custom cookie with the couple's names iced on it and wrapped in a clear sleeve, tied with a ribbon, are often the most popular. So is a wrapped chocolate. For the most part, wine glasses, hot chocolate bombs, even little bottles of wine are often left behind at the end of the night. Coasters, once popular, are no longer of interest. Some couples decide to donate to a local pet or other charity and announce this in some way at the wedding. Usually there is a framed announcement that may say: "In lieu of favors, we have made a contribution to the Humane Society." You get the idea!

ProTip: *If you want to have favors and they are not an edible item like a cookie or chocolate, I suggest having them in baskets, lined up at the sign-in table, or scattered around the centerpiece of each table. Consider ordering one half or two thirds of your guest count in this case, and you'll likely have less waste at the end of the evening.*

Memory tables are often set up somewhere near the sign-in table, and can include framed photos of passed loved ones, and any tributes the family may wish to express. Usually there are candles enclosed in votive cups or clear cylinders, and a small centerpiece or vase of flowers.

The last thing to think about regarding tables is where you and the love of your life will sit once you enter the reception. A sweetheart table is typically a small round table, set for the two of you. It is usually placed close to the dance floor, and with family tables on either side. The advantage to this is that your bridal party can sit with their family or spouses. If you choose a long grouping of rectangular tables for your entire bridal party, that is also fine. Think about these formations, and how you will decorate either the sweetheart or the long bridal table.

Sometimes a venue can lend itself to decor. Barns and botanic gardens are often beautiful enough and need little embellishment. Some venues will have added touches, including props or their own vintage signage. If you choose one of these reception locations, consider saving money by limiting yourself to simple centerpieces of seasonal flowers and signage.

Speaking of signage (which can be overwhelming), it's best to work on this area throughout the months before your big day. Think about what you can create at the entrance to your ceremony or the reception area.

An example would be "Welcome to the Wedding of Ashley and William." Many couples also have the "unplugged" announcement (limiting phone use and photo-taking), either at the bottom of the welcome sign, or in their program. A plain welcome sign can be transported from the church to the reception by a family member or your wedding coordinator.

If you are creating signature cocktails, you might want framed signage for the bar area advertising your drinks. Dessert or cookie tables can also be opportunities for labeling. It is a nice touch to designate nut- and gluten-free or vegan specialties, or to recognize aunts and other relatives who may have baked for your occasion.

To recap, signage options can include:
- ❏ Welcome Sign
- ❏ "Unplugged" Sign
- ❏ Signature Cocktails
- ❏ Desserts
- ❏ Memory Table

I've seen many weddings where it seems like there's been a hard time with setting limits. Couples are bombarded with ideas in social media, and it is hard to narrow down choices. A wedding is a once in a lifetime event and I know how hard it can be to set personal limits on spending and embellishments. You can go to wedding flea markets, or scout social media sites where brides sell off their wedding decor for a fraction of the cost. But before you get stars in your eyes over gold charger plates and electric candles, think through the look you really want. I've seen large vans pull up to many wedding venues, and the unloading and decorating go on for hours. Less can be more. Look carefully... and you will likely see the beauty of your reception room and the wealth of what is already there for your use.

Notes

COUNTDOWN TO HAPPILY EVER AFTER

Your dream come true is about to unfold!

We are down to the last month or a few weeks before your wedding day! I'm sure you are super excited, placing the finishing touches on your decor, gathering RSVPs, and finalizing any vendor requests for information.

Here's a checklist for the month leading up to your wedding day:

- Fill out DJ, photographer, and any other paperwork that is due.
- Finalize any payment deadlines.
- Have final alterations and pick up your dress.
- Make sure you have two pairs of shoes for the big day — one dressy and one comfortable.
- Touch base with the officiant. Confirm your ceremony details and arrival times for rehearsal and wedding day.
- Relay rehearsal time and place details to your bridal party. Confirm dinner number to your rehearsal dinner restaurant.
- Finalize RSVP reservations and call, text, or email any guests who have not responded.

- ❐ Confirm when you need to have your final number of guests to your caterer.
- ❐ Find out the timings for wedding day drop-offs such as flowers at the church, and when your DJ arrives at the reception venue.
- ❐ Ask if you can leave anything at the church/venue after rehearsal, such as programs, bubbles, and candles.
- ❐ Make a list aligning your bridesmaids with the groomsmen, and the order you want them to go down the aisle.
- ❐ Make a list of family members you want in your first two rows of seating at the ceremony.
- ❐ Make a list of the photos you want taken of your family after the ceremony.
- ❐ Acquire your marriage license.
- ❐ Pick up your wedding bands.
- ❐ Make your exit plan for the night of the wedding. Line up help with boxing up decor and loading into vehicles.

ProTip: *Some of your bridal party may be working on the day of the rehearsal, so remember to reach out to everyone ahead of time to make sure they can make the time slot you are considering. It's best to finalize times when you've heard from your entire party.*

One of the most common issues I hear is about guests who fail to RSVP. Whether you have a wedding website, or response cards to mail back, there will always be a few people who have not responded by your deadline. My answer to this concern is always the same: you must get a hold of these individuals one way or another and ask if they are coming. The Mindful Bride is not resentful about doing this, understanding that people are busy and yes, they can forget. Try the following line: *"I'm sorry to bother you, but our final number is due to the caterer, and we wouldn't want you to arrive and not have a seat assignment for dinner."*

There are wedding events where an extra table is placed for the people who fail to respond. You can do this, but you must include (and budget for) the six or eight dinners that will need to be set. And your venue or day-of coordinator should be informed of the table, so that any unplanned guests can be directed there.

Final Walk-Through

If you have a planner or coordinator, they should accompany you to your reception venue to review the final details of your wedding day. There should be no charge from the venue to do this walk-through, and frankly they should encourage it. This should occur approximately three to four weeks before your wedding day. You can arrange this visit, or your coordinator can arrange it by asking for your availability and emailing the venue (you should be copied on all correspondence). Once this walk-through has occurred, your venue or wedding coordinator should contact all vendors and add their arrival times to the timeline (see Day-of Wedding timeline below for details). The final timeline should be mailed to the venue and vendors on the Sunday or Monday before the wedding weekend.

Here's a checklist for the final walkthrough:

- ❒ Go over the floor plan of your cocktail hour and reception. Afterwards, the venue should be able to email both you and the coordinator a final layout.
- ❒ Add any extra tables — memorial, sign-in, gifts, desserts, etc. — you may need.
- ❒ Ask when boxes of decor and other items can be dropped off.
- ❒ Clarify who is providing tablecloths and what time they will be setting them on the morning of the wedding.
- ❒ Remember to determine if you want a sweetheart table or a long bridal table and how the tablecloths will cover each one.
- ❒ Go over the proposed timeline making additions or corrections as needed.
- ❒ If there is a cookie or dessert table, clarify how and when the treats will be delivered and stored.
- ❒ Your day-of wedding coordinator should ask to be onsite at least two to three hours ahead, to greet vendors and set decor.
- ❒ Find out where the vendors usually eat, if they are not eating in the main area.
- ❒ If you have any handicapped guests, ask where they can park and safely enter the building. Ask about the restrooms for them as well.
- ❒ Ask if there is a room where the bridal party can be kept aside from the cocktail and reception areas, before they are announced.
- ❒ If you are not hiring a planner or coordinator, ask the

venue if they have a coordinator that can follow your timeline and assist your bridal party.

❐ Find out the venue's closing rules and if all your decor, etc. needs to be removed that night.

Rehearsal

If you have a day-of coordinator or planner, they should accompany you to the rehearsal. Your coordinator should contact the minister or officiant prior to the rehearsal, just to introduce themselves. This isn't always possible, but it's nice to do so.

If there is a ceremony coordinator at your venue or church, they will usually line up your bridal party in the order you have given them. The procession should be practiced twice. The officiant will go over the ceremony details with the couple. Your day-of coordinator or planner can do the same things as a ceremony coordinator, if there is not one provided.

Here's a checklist for rehearsal:

❐ If someone from the bridal party is absent at rehearsal, use a fill-in such as a spouse. Don't wait too long for anyone who is late.

❐ Bring anything you are allowed to leave there, such as the programs, candles, bubbles, etc.

❐ Confirm the arrival time on the wedding day, which should be at least 30 minutes before the ceremony starts.

❐ Know where the restrooms are.

❐ See if there is a holding area where the bridal party can stay until the ceremony starts.

- ❐ Ask if groomsmen want to escort guests in the twenty or thirty minutes before the ceremony starts.
- ❐ Determine if you will have a receiving line, or if you'll dismiss guests after the ceremony by rows.
- ❐ See if there is a special room for parents with children, if you are inviting them.
- ❐ If you have any handicapped guests, ask where they should be placed.
- ❐ Have a plan for blocking off the first one or two rows of seating for guests.
- ❐ Make sure the family you want in the first one or two pews/rows are aware you want them to sit there. People will not always assume they are special!

Day-of Wedding Timeline

A *day-of wedding* timeline is one of the most important tools for an overall calm wedding day. If you have hired a planner or day-of coordinator, they should assist you in creating it.

Here is a basic day-of wedding timeline:

8:00 AM	Wake up at the hotel, have breakfast with the bridesmaids.
9:00 AM	Hair and makeup stylists arrive. Photographer arrives.
11:00 AM	Time for bride and bridesmaids to get dressed! Groomsmen dress at a separate hotel or residence. Make sure the bridal party has a hearty snack or lunch wherever they are.
12:00 PM	Shuttle arrives for the bridal party.

12:30 PM	Arrive at the destination for First Look photos.
1:30 PM	Photography ends, ride to the ceremony.
2:00 PM	Arrive at church or venue for ceremony. Use the restroom and freshen makeup and hair before walking down the aisle.
2:30 PM	Ceremony (estimated for 30 minutes)
3:00 PM	Ceremony ends. Guests move to the venue. Post-ceremony photography with family.
3:30 PM	Cocktail Hour at venue.
4:30 PM	Announcements + First Dance + Cut the Cake + Toasts (two or three) + Blessing
5:00 PM	Dinner served.
6:00 PM	Cookie table or desserts served. Dance floor opens!
7:00 PM	Mother/Son and Father/Daughter Dance. Place the card box in a secure location.
8:00 PM	Dancing for all.
9:50 PM	Last dance.
10:00 PM	Clean up decor, etc. and load cars.

A few things on the timeline that need further explanation:

Have Food Available

Make sure everyone in the bridal party eats something on the day of the wedding. Be mindful that all of you may or may not eat at the cocktail hour because this is often when photos are taken. And the bridal party is typically announced at the opening of the reception, which is a long time to wait to eat! Incorporate food into the wedding day morning and have a bag of protein bars or snacks (avoid chocolate coated things as they are too messy) and bottles of water that can be in your shuttle or limo.

A First Look

A First Look is something you can consider if you are nervous about walking down the aisle or want a more leisurely day with plenty of time for photography. Your coordinator or photographer can help you arrange a time and spot for you and your fiancé to first see each other. Whatever option you may choose, a First Look before or at the ceremony, is fine and completely up to you both.

Your Card Box

After dinner, it is best to lock up your card box (or other receptacle for guests to place their cards for your gift) in a safe place. Sometimes a venue will provide a locked office, or if you trust the locale, lock the box inside of your parent's car trunk. People can do impulsive things when they drink, and it is best not to provide the temptation of a box full of money or checks. Also, make sure the card box is moved from a cocktail area to the main room when the reception begins. Never place a card box near an exit door or isolate it from where it can't be observed.

Toasts

Usually, the best man and maid of honor will give a toast. This can sometimes be a tricky situation, especially if they've already had a bit to drink. Some toasts can be long, not too flattering, or downright embarrassing. As a coordinator, I will sometimes speak to both the best man and maid of honor, asking them to keep it brief and well intentioned. Ask your coordinator for advice if you feel the speeches could be too personal.

Parents will occasionally make speeches, welcoming guests and speaking of their love for the couple. These tend to be well scripted and heartwarming.

Lastly, try to confirm the length of all toasts in advance so that the timeline you communicate to all coordinators, caterers, vendors, et al. remains accurate.

Day-of Wedding Kit

Most planners/coordinators will carry a "day-of" kit, so ask them if they do. It should include the following:

- ☐ Hair Spray
- ☐ Tide or other stain stick
- ☐ Tampons
- ☐ Motrin or Tylenol
- ☐ Tape
- ☐ Scissors
- ☐ Floral wire and tape
- ☐ Corsage and regular pins
- ☐ Ribbon

On one wedding morning, I happened to have fresh basil and mint in my herb garden. I decided to take a mason jar of the herbs to my farm wedding. It turned out that the groom did not have a boutonniere, so I offered to make him one. It is visible in the photos from this wedding, and I'm proud that my flower shop background (it was my first job in high school) provided me with the skill to create or fix just about any floral need. Since then, I've always carried floral tape and wire in my kit.

Your wedding planner or coordinator is your liaison, confidant, and support person during your planning process and especially leading up to your day of wedding. Don't hesitate to contact them, even with the smallest question. The Mindful Bride is a blessing to any coordinator, and they want to make sure your wishes are met. Never worry about burdening them. They are there for you.

Notes

_____

_____

_____

_____

_____

_____

_____

_____

_____

_____

_____

THROUGH THE EYES
OF A BRIDE

Stay in the moment as much as you can!
It will fly by in an instant!

The big day is here! How are you feeling? Excited, a bit nervous maybe? You've done a great job planning your day! You have a dream team of a bridal party, and your vendors are lined up, ready to make this your Best Day Ever. Time to enjoy the ride!

There are things you can remember to do on this special day, but if you forget it all and live in the moment, that is the most important thing! Remember that the goal of this little book, *The Mindful Bride*, is for you to have a calm wedding day!

As the cherry on top, I'm going to give you a few last pointers to make today even more calm. Read on, dear bride, and know that I am with you today!

Eat

Yes, you must eat something or nibble throughout the day. Avoid colored drinks that may spill on your dress or attire — think ginger ale, white wine, champagne, water. Try to eat breakfast but if that's too hard, then eat around 11:00 AM or Noon. Remember your bag of protein bars and water for the limo or shuttle!

If something happens, just ride with it!

Something is bound to happen, but you may or may not find out about it! If it's regarding you, let others (like your coordinator or bridesmaids!) help you take care of it. Let them solve the issue while you get your hair and make-up done! If something happens to someone else, let your dream team handle it!

Live in the Moment

I've said this before but now you get to do it. Your mind may race to the details of the day but try to stay centered. Repeat a personal mantra or do some deep breathing. When you walk down the aisle, look ahead at your beloved, and feel every moment of your walk towards them. Listen to the words of your officiant. Notice the interior of the church, or the sky if you are outside. Feel the words you are saying if you are reading your vows.

Try to see your reception area

If your cocktail hour is in a different area than the reception, see if the venue coordinator (or your own coordinator) can get you into the room before everyone else sees it. Take a moment or two to admire your hard work that has come to fruition!

Have a few minutes, just the two of you

If you can sneak away for a few minutes, hug, kiss, and share a few private moments.

Stay with each other throughout the reception.

You will each be pulled in different directions by family and friends but do your best to hold hands and stay together. This is your day, for the two of you, so remember to be present as a couple as much as possible.

Dance and enjoy yourself!

Have fun, relax, don't fuss over any details, and certainly don't get caught up in any drama. If you need anything, go to your coordinator, Maid of Honor, Best Man, or your designated problem solver of the day. Don't spend more than a minute or two on any one issue. Make a decision, if you must, and then move on. Back to dancing!

Let others do the clean-up

This is what your dream team is for … and your vendors. At the end of the evening, let them do the bulk of the work. Take off for the after party, the hotel, or wherever you can get a bit of rest!

Best Wishes
for a Fabulous
Wedding Day!

AFTER THE WEDDING: THANK YOU'S AND BEYOND

Gratitude, reflection, and navigating life after "'I do."

How was your Big Day? Hopefully it was all you dreamed about! Magical, wonderful, thrilling, and *simply beautiful.* Please know how truly happy I am for you! You did it!

It might be a lovely keepsake to write your thoughts in a journal or other paper memento. Think about the little miracles, the love of your family and guests, and the special parts of the day. Once written, these are the words that you will reflect back on and cherish.

If anything went slightly awry, don't obsess over it. Truthfully, no wedding goes completely by plan. The Mindful Bride allows for the natural unfolding of the day and the grace that comes along with it.

The rush of excitement over the last weeks or months may keep your adrenaline going for some time. At some point, you may feel quite exhausted. This is the time to rest, relax, and enjoy time with your life partner. Ease into married life and allow yourself ample space to come down from a year's worth of planning.

A couple of weeks later, there are things that you can do to wrap up your wedding journey and begin a newlywed life. The first is to take stock of your gifts, monetary and otherwise. It doesn't matter if you choose standard thank you type stationary or create something special all your own. If your photographer delivers a few early digital images, create a special thank you note with a wedding photo, or even a postcard.

Please don't neglect to write thank you's. The longer you wait, the worse this task will become. There is a standard etiquette that allows for up to three months to do this, but it's best to get the task completed as soon as the wedding dust settles. Enlist the aid of your spouse or even a close friend (yes, anything to get them done) to write, address, stamp, and do whatever you need help with. Break it down to five a night, five days a week, and soon they'll be finished!

Here's an easy checklist of other things to think about:

- ❐ Are you keeping your dress? Check online reviews and find a good dry cleaner to preserve it. Some alternatives include donating it to a charity, or to an angel seamstress who will make a dress for babies that have passed. Or you can sell it in a local online wedding community after you have it cleaned.
- ❐ If you are changing your name, now is the time to initiate the paperwork. You will need to visit a Social Security office, and once your new name is granted, change your bank accounts, driver's license, insurance, etc.

❏ You can preserve your bouquet too. Check online for local vendors or ask your online wedding community for recommendations.

❏ Have a ton of leftover decor? Consider consignment, donation, or selling it online in a local wedding community. Don't have huge expectations. Sales of used decor rarely match what you paid. But you'll get a little something and another bride will benefit from your generosity.

❏ Create your wedding album and order prints. You will receive many images to choose from so take your time. Photographers use the best companies to print their images so if you want a large photo to frame and hang, splurge and use their services.

❏ Wrap your cake tier and save it. Don't use foil. Wrap it in several layers of plastic wrap and place in an airtight bag or container. Label it so it doesn't get mistaken for something else. Many bakeries now offer a small extra cake a year later, so if yours does, take advantage of it.

❏ Send your vendors some love. Write online reviews about the great things they did. They will appreciate every word.

Last but not least, take the time to do things in a calm and organized manner. Don't push yourself too hard. The Mindful Bride knows that slow and steady wins the race.

Bonus Section

COOKIE TABLES!

From Dough to Display:
The Art and Science of
Creating the Perfect Cookie Table

The wedding cookie table is most commonly found around Pittsburgh, PA and Youngstown, OH. It is largely attributed to the immigrant populations that brought their traditions and recipes with them when they began a new life in America.

Cookie tables are immensely popular. Whether you have family members do the baking, or hire outside help, your guests will love a good cookie table!

Here are some commonly asked questions and helpful answers:

How many cookies should we bake per guest?

When you have a *solid idea of your RSVP count*, six to eight cookies per person is plenty. For example, if you are expecting 100 guests, 50 dozen cookies are ideal (100 x 6 = 600, divided by 12 = 50). More than that is fine, but make sure you save your transport containers as you may be taking some home.

What types of cookies are most popular?

Ethnic specialties such as pizzelles, baklava, kolaczki, and nut rolls are big hits. American favorites like caramel cups, buckeyes, and lady locks (a fusion of American and ethnic roots) are often the first to go! Thumbprints and mini cupcakes, with the icing color matching the main wedding color, beautify the table and link it to the couple.

Should we open the cookie table from cocktail hour on, or after dinner?

If the cookie table will be the dessert instead of a wedding cake, then wait until after dinner. When you initially set the cookie table, cover the entire spread with netting. People will respect it. Ask the event/catering staff to remove the netting after dinner.

If you have more than ten cookies per person, I suggest allowing guests to nibble from the cookie table during cocktail hour. Why? Because otherwise you may be eating cookies the following Christmas! The strategy for having them out at cocktail hour is to have only cocktail napkins and small disposable plates available. Bring the take-home containers out around 8:00 PM, or as soon as the guests are through the buffet line.

What is the best take-home container?

In my opinion, the square, clear plastic clam shell design that snaps shut is best. They are most secure and can be recycled. Order one half of your guest count in take home containers (100 guests = 50 containers).

Should I pay my venue, caterer, or outside business to set up my cookie table?

Without question, my answer here is YES. Many venues or caterers are now charging a small fee per person to do this. It is worth every penny. You and your family will be too busy on the day of your wedding to worry about this detail. Give the set-up person any decorative props ahead of time and work out all the specifics in advance.

Can I ask my venue to store cookies a couple of days ahead?

Yes again! Ask your venue if you can drop off cookies a day or two in advance. Have the cookies in secure boxes or containers, marked with the family or couple's name. If certain cookies need to be refrigerated, ask ahead of time if there will be room in the kitchen's refrigerator (not freezer!).

Should I label the different cookie types?

This is up to you. Most people recognize different cookie types or can usually figure them out (that's the fun of tasting!). Giving credit on individual place cards to your family members who baked takes time, but it's a special touch.

Should there be Nut-Free and Gluten-Free choices?

As this is an important part of life today, having some gluten-free and nut-free choices are thoughtful. Just make sure that they get labeled and stay separated. Talk to your caterer in advance about this important request so that they are aware and set the table accordingly.

My family wants to set up the cookie table. How much time should I allow?

If your family is setting up the cookie table, allow three to four hours to tray and set up 50 dozen cookies. Remember to pay attention to nut- and gluten-free options as mentioned above. Lady locks and cream cheese-filled cookies also need special care. These should be placed as close as possible to serving time. Save all boxes. Store them under the tables if they are skirted. You can easily pack and transport any leftovers and props at the end of the evening.

What can I do to make my cookie table special?

Venues and caterers will cover the tables with tablecloths and sometimes use pedestals to heighten individual trays. If you want to provide special pedestals, vintage plates or heirloom trays, this will enhance the look of your cookie table. Make sure you have your name on the bottom of everything. You can coordinate your table with all silver, gold, or vintage trays ... or make a mismatched combination. Be creative!

Sprinkle wrapped chocolates around the table for a delicious effect. Have signs such as "We know yinz are here for the cookie table." (Pittsburgh-natives will understand!) There are even platters you can order that explain the history of the cookie table. Order a cookie cutter with an imprint of the wedding couple and use it to make sugar or other flat cookies.

Enjoy the baking! Recruit friends and family to help or hire a baker. Read up on what you can bake and freeze ahead of time. Join the Pittsburgh Wedding Cookie Table Community, where thousands of people share their best recipes and help others with cookie table questions.

I Want a Cookie Table!

_____

_____

_____

_____

_____

_____

_____

_____

_____

_____

_____

_____

_____

_____

_____

_____

_____

_____

_____

_____

_____

_____

_____

Thank You

Thank you for reading my book and for your desire to be "The Mindful Bride." You made it through all the planning and your special day with calmness and compassion. I wish you great health and happiness in your married life!

With Love,

Joanne

Memories

_____

_____

_____

_____

_____

_____

_____

_____

_____

_____

_____

_____

_____

_____

_____

_____

_____

_____

_____

_____

_____

_____

Photo by Jessica Lubert Photography

Still a bride after all these years!

Author
Joanne Jamis Cain

Once upon a time, I opened a coffee shop. It was an homage to my favorite brewed beverage as I had been a coffee lover since my early teens. I used to spend summers with my "yiayia" (Greek for "grandmother") and she always had one of those old fashioned metal pots on the stove, perking away with fresh coffee. I am still a coffee lover to this day!

During most of my seven years as owner of Cappuccino City in Sewickley, I served on the board of the Sewickley Chamber of Commerce. During my board tenure, I began to assist with numerous events, primarily community-oriented ones.

After I sold my business, I worked for the Pittsburgh Parks Conservancy as the first manager of the newly renovated Schenley Park Visitor Center. I assisted the Conservancy in every aspect of this "jewel in the park" — café, gifts, visitor services, and event rentals. At that time, the internet was not what it is today, so I was fortunate to employ local university interns who helped develop the event side of the business. We basically formed the rental protocols from the ground up, including the rates, rules, and even vendor suggestions. The Visitor Center is still a popular choice for rentals to this day!

After I left the Center, the Executive Director of Rodef Shalom Congregation, Jeff Herzog, saw my potential. We were in the same service organization, and one day he asked me if I was looking for any full-time opportunities. My interest was piqued so I called him and set up a time for us to meet.

When he interviewed me, he confidently said, "You are perfect for the job."

Because I had no idea what the job was, I asked somewhat quizzically, "What is the job?" He simply replied, "Events Coordinator." I told him I didn't know a thing about Judaism, but he reassured me with his answer: "Everyone will be very patient with you while you learn." And very patient they were, with a Christian woman who had never set foot in a synagogue before!

In the five years I was with the congregation, I planned just about every bar/bat mitzvah, wedding, life cycle event, and non-profit fundraiser on the calendar. I wrote the logistics and timeline, interfaced with vendors, and handed down details to the kitchen and maintenance crew. My job at the time did not require me to be on-site on weekends, so I was not the one executing the actual events. But every Monday, I walked into work, eager to ask the crew how the events of the weekend went!

After a few years, families started asking me to come on the day of their weddings to supervise and oversee the details. This is when I officially started doing "day-of" wedding coordination. Then one summer, I assisted a friend at her farm wedding. Apparently, the farm owner was so impressed that she asked me back the next summer! So, I moonlighted the following year and did about six barn weddings. That's when I really fell in love with weddings.

My background in sales, customer service, business, and events led me to start another business when my mother's health began to decline. I left full-time employment and started Katherine's Daughter Events. At the time, my personal story blog was named "Katherine's Daughter," so it felt natural to name my business similarly and to continue to honor my mother, Katherine. I am always proud to say that my mom taught me everything I know about hospitality. The business honors her legacy and is a tribute to the timeless hostess she always was.

ALSO BY
Joanne Jamis Cain

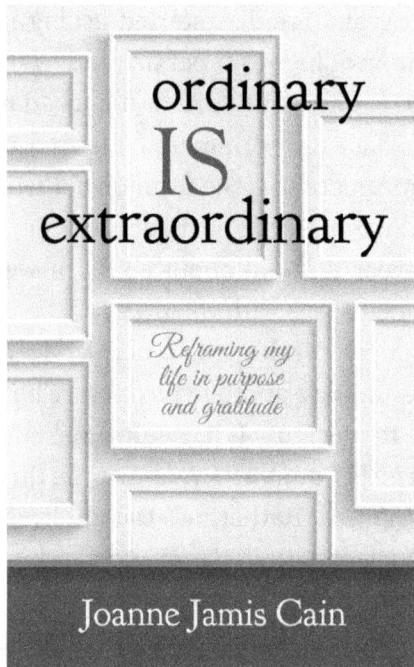

ordinary
IS
extraordinary

Reframing my
life in purpose
and gratitude

Joanne Jamis Cain

Ordinary is Extraordinary is for anyone who wishes for a more fulfilling life. Our lives are busy and oftentimes we get caught up in a frantic pace. Through sharing her personal experience, strength and hope, Joanne Jamis Cain makes us aware of the grace to be found in everyday life. A recovering perfectionist, Joanne encourages simplicity and mindful living instead of worry and impatience. Through her stories of grace, love, and parking spaces, she tells us how reframing our experiences helps us recognize the blessings in our lives. Embracing a life of purpose and gratitude is a game changer. Joanne's debut inspirational book will motivate you to look inward to find meaning and purpose in your life.